ANOINTING
THE AUTHORIZATION TO BREAK EVERY YOKE

SVEIN BERGE

ANOINTING
THE AUTHORIZATION TO BREAK EVERY YOKE

Rhema Publications

ANOINTING
THE AUTHORIZATION TO BREAK EVERY YOKE

Copyright © Svein Berge, 2016

ALL RIGHTS RESERVED

ISBN 978-0-9574620-6-9

First Published in Great Britain in 2016 by
Rhema Publications Ltd,
67-68 Hatton Garden - New House
London EC1N 8JY

Printed in Great Britain

ACKNOWLEDGEMENTS

First of all, I would like to give a warm thank you to everyone who has been a part of making this book possible. Special thanks to Dr. Régine Mfoumou from Rhema Publications who has helped me to stick within time limits and overall has made the professional publishing of this book possible.

A great thank you to all of you who, over a period of many years, have acknowledged and faithfully listened to my teachings. Also, a great thank you to all who helped me with the homemade booklets through financial support, providing a laser printer, buying, reading and recommending them.

But above all, thank you to God Himself who gave His own Son for our salvation. This book is all about serving Him. Therefore, it is with great confidence we dare to declare this book written and published in Jesus' name!

West Kensington, London, February 2016.

TABLE OF CONTENT

INTRODUCTION

Sunday, 14th March 1999. Morning service in La Paz.

After preaching, I ministered to the people, as I operated in the gifts of the Holy Spirit. You could feel the anointing in a very strong way. As I was ministering to the people, I heard somebody praying, and for some reason, it sounded peculiar. I went towards the one was praying, laid my hands on the person and said with a loud voice: 'Go in the name of Jesus Christ!'

Immediately, the person fell on the floor and started to shake and partially move his body like a snake. After a while, he became relaxed and quiet. When we had a chat with him afterwards, he said that it was as if something had left him and he felt lighter. It turned out that he had gone through severe things as a very young boy, which seemed to be the reason for the manifestations that happened to him as he was ministered to.

After this, we interceded and ministered to people for some hours. The prayer line never seemed to end.

CHAPTER 1
THE BIBLICAL PRINCIPLE OF AUTHORIZATION

To obtain victory for the sake of the Gospel, for biblical church growth and to be effective in Christian work and ministry, God-given authority is a must. When someone is authorized, they automatically have authority.

It is crucial to clarify that when the word 'authority' is used, it does not refer to 'authority' in its common connotation or by its secular meaning, namely the use of controlling and manipulative technique for the purpose of subduing and thereby abusing other people. The latter has nothing to do with the biblical, God-given authority this book is dealing with. Both Jesus and Peter warn us against it:

> *But Jesus called them to Himself and said to them, 'You know that those who are considered rulers over the Gentiles lord it over them, and their great ones exercise authority over them. Yet it shall not be so among you; but whoever desires to become great among you shall be your servant. And whoever of you desires to be first shall be slave of all. For even the Son of Man did not come to be served, but to serve, and to give His life a ransom for many.' (Mark 10:42-45, NKJV).*

> *Shepherd the flock of God which is among you, serving as overseers, not by compulsion but willingly, not for dishonest gain but eagerly; nor as being lords over those entrusted to you, but being examples to the flock; and*

So, the expressions 'authority', 'God-given authority', or 'divine authority' that are used in this book are not, in any way, meant to exalt man. On the contrary, they are used as a distinction of our own, natural, non-crucified authority that we are born with as the latter form of authority must not take the place of God's authority through us.

When we deal with people, we certainly have no right to operate in or to exercise our own authority. Only God's authority must be exercised. The place where our own natural authority belongs is on the cross and in the tomb with Christ. Through the resurrection of Christ, we participate in His divine authority.

Unfortunately, even though God authorizes us, it is still possible for us to operate in this authority without love. This is of course not sound. Our inner man and spirit must be kept in a sound condition. We need a spirit of authority, but we also need the spirit of love. On the one hand, authority without love is like a sounding cymbal. On the other hand, if we have love without authority, we are not effective. Love is the greatest of all. But contrarily to common opinion, love is not a universal medicine that can substitute for other things like faith, power, authority, confession and preaching, etc. Love will never fail in its purpose. But love will not do it all. Love is helpless without the necessary tools, abilities and power required or needed to express that love.

> *Though I speak with the tongues of men and of angels, but have not love, I have become sounding brass or a clanging cymbal. And though I have the gift of prophecy, and understand all mysteries and all knowledge, and though I have all faith, so that I could remove mountains, but have not love, I am nothing. And though I bestow all my goods to feed the poor, and though I give my body to be burned, but have not love, it profits me nothing. Love suffers long and is kind; love does not envy; love does not parade itself, is not puffed up; does not behave rudely, does not seek its own, is not provoked, thinks no evil; does not rejoice in iniquity, but rejoices in the truth; bears all things, believes all things, hopes all things, endures all things. Love never fails. But whether there are prophecies, they will fail; whether there are tongues, they will cease; whether there is knowledge, it will vanish away.*
> *(1 Corinthians 13:1-8, NKJV).*

Overall, we are not referring to 'authorization' or 'authority' as a personality trait or as a mystical (invisible) substance. We approach the words 'authority' and 'authorization' as plain legal terms. Please be aware that we are tackling the topic of authority and not the topic of power here!

Natural authority, which we are born with, must be reckoned as 'crucified' with Christ. Those who are authorized by God and given authority from Him must not allow themselves to operate in their own natural authority. When natural authority substitutes God-given, divine and spiritual authority, it blocks God's true authority from manifesting on earth through the Church. In the Book of Acts, we find that tremendous results were obtained for the kingdom of God and that the early Church was uttermost effective in proclaiming the Gospel. The key to these things was the kind of Spiritual authority that comes from God. They had authority in the spiritual realm.

Indeed, Apostle Paul and his co-workers were given authority:

> *I may seem to be boasting too much about **the authority given to us by the Lord**. But our authority builds you up; it doesn't tear you down. So I will not be ashamed of **using my authority**. (2 Corinthians 10:8, NLT).*

There are times when God-given authority must be exercised, or 'used':

> *You may think I overstate **the authority he gave me**, but I'm not backing off. Every bit of my commitment is for the purpose of building you up, after all, not tearing you down. (2 Corinthians 10:8, MSG).*

> *For even if I should boast somewhat more about **our authority, which the Lord gave us** for edification and not for your destruction, I shall not be ashamed.*
> *(2 Corinthians 10:8, NKJV).*

> *That's why I write these things before I come to you. Then when I do come, I won't have to be hard on you when I **use** my authority. **The Lord gave me the authority** to build you up. He didn't give it to me to tear you down.*
> *(2 Corinthians 13:10, NIRV).*

In the above examples, the authority that was given relates to building up and ministering to the church: they had God-given authority in the church; they had authority among God's people.

Let's compare this with the following verse:

> *And God has appointed these **in the church**: First apostles, Second prophets, Third teachers, **After that** miracles, then gifts of healings, helps, administrations, varieties of tongues. (1 Corinthians 12:28, NKJV).*

1. Apostles
2. Prophets
3. Teachers

The first three ministries mentioned here are typical governing ministries. Because of their governing aspect, we may describe them as offices. 'Ministry' is gift-based whilst 'office' is authority-based (hence the expression 'governing'). As an example, the ministry of a prophet requires the spiritual gift to prophesy. The gift of a teacher requires the divine (God-given) gift to teach. Thus, on the one hand, having the ministry of a prophet or the ministry of a teacher does not in any way guarantee that you have a governing function in the body of Christ. But, on the other hand, to have a governing office, such as the office of an apostle or the office of a teacher, will, of course, require that you have a ministry, and additionally possess the gifts necessary to operate in that particular ministry.

Moreover, the expressions 'first', 'second' and 'third' strongly indicate their level of God-given authority in the body of Christ. This said, these first three ministries are not based on formal authority, but on spiritual authority. In other words, these three ministries are not obtained by the choice or the election of men. Absolutely not! They are given and authorized by the Holy Spirit Himself.

Thus, it is crucial to note the fact that, based on 1 Corinthians 12:28, when the Bible says (first) apostles, (second) prophets and (third) teachers, it is obvious from the context that it refers to apostles, prophets and teachers as ministries here. Even though they are *governing* ministries it refers to ministries as the apostolic, the prophetic and the teaching *ministries*. From, the Bible we read this:

> *And God has appointed these **in the church**: First apostles, Second prophets, Third teachers, **After that** miracles, then gifts of healings, helps, administrations, varieties of tongues. (1 Corinthians 12:28, NKJV).*

It should be obvious now, from what we have explained above, that when the Bible says: "after that, miracles, then gifts of healing" and so on, that it refers to ministries, like 'ministry of miracles', 'ministry of healing', and so on. When it also says 'varieties of tongues' here, it, therefore, doesn't refer to the kind of tongues that are for private use. Instead, it refers to tongues

meant for public use. This is a ministry in the church. For this kind
of tongues to operate, it will evidently require that the same person
or another person who has the gift to interpret these tongues be
present. It is of crucial important to understand that there is a
difference between tongues as a public ministry and tongues for
private, personal use. Let us now look into the next verses:

> *All are not apostles, are they? All are not prophets, are*
> *they? All are not teachers, are they? All are not workers*
> *of miracles, are they? All do not have gifts of healings, do*
> *they? All do not speak with tongues, do they?*
> *(1 Corinthians 12:29-30, NASB).*

As this is a continuation of the previous verse, it should be
clear that based on the context, when it says "all do not, speak
with tongues" it solely refers to tongues for public use.
Consequently, this Bible verse (1 Corinthians 12:30) does not, in
any way, disqualify anyone from speaking in tongues when they
are baptized in, or filled with the Holy Spirit.

We then have a problem here: in today's modern church, we
want what comes after, without wanting what comes first. We
want miracles, healing and tongues like in the Book of Acts,
without having to accept apostles, prophets and teachers. It seems
that we very much have the key here or the so-called 'missing
link' when it comes to a breakthrough in the area of miraculous

healings, and God confirming His Word like in the Book of Acts. Therefore, we may conclude this:

- Cause: apostles, prophets and teachers (1 Corinthians 5:28a).

- Effect: *Miracles*, then gifts of *healings*, helps, *administrations*, varieties of *tongues* (1 Corinthians 5:28b).

In other words, the cause is the three offices that are mentioned. The gifts (or the gifts in proper operation) are the effect of these three offices (in operation).

With the expression 'ministry gifts', we actually mean the people themselves (individuals) that Christ Himself gave as gifts to us (Ephesians 4:11), the Church, after His ascension. These [that He gave as gifts] people are the apostles, the prophets, the evangelists, the pastors and the teachers mentioned in Ephesians 4:11. If we say no to, and do not want something that (as in this case) is a gift from Christ Himself, how do we think He may feel? We find it reasonable to believe that it will make Him feel grieved.

If we exclude any of these ministry gifts, we also miss out the specific gifts and manifestations of these gifts that God has invested in each one of the five ministries mentioned above. Obviously, we should accept and receive all the five groups of people (ministry gifts) that are mentioned in Ephesians 4:11.

As we can read on the passage above, these five gifts (ministers) were given after Christ's ascension, not before. The Bible says that "to you *they* are given":

CHAPTER II
APPLICATION OF THE AUTHORIZATION

2.1. Authorized by sending

Below are some Bible verses referring to being authorized by sending:

> *Then He called His twelve disciples together and gave them power and authority over all demons, and to cure diseases.* ***He sent them*** *to preach the kingdom of God and to heal the sick. (Luke 9:1-2, NKJV).*

> *After these things the Lord appointed seventy others also,* ***and sent them*** *two by two before His face into every city and place where He Himself was about to go. (Luke 10:1, NKJV).*

If they had not been *sent* by *Him*, nothing would have worked. There would be no casting out of demons, no healing of diseases and no effective preaching of the Kingdom.

> *There was* ***a man*** *sent* ***from God****, whose name was John. (John 1:6, NKJV).*

> *Jesus said to them, 'My food is to do the will of* ***Him who*** *sent* ***Me****, and to finish His work.' (John 4:34, NKJV).*

> *As You sent Me into the world, I also* ***have*** *sent* ***them*** *into the world. (John 17:18, NKJV).*

> *So Jesus said to them again, 'Peace to you! As* ***the Father has sent Me, I also*** *send* ***you****.' (John 20:21, NKJV).*

Of course, there is no reference here in relation to being sent by men, but rather being sent by God, which implies that preaching without being sent will manifest no authority. To be more precise, no one is allowed to preach the Word of God or the Gospel without divine authorization; only the redeemed children of God are authorized to declare His Word:

Therefore, those who have not experienced salvation and are not born again are not licensed to spread God's Word and testimony.

The power to heal sicknesses, as well as the power to cast out unclean spirits, comes along with the sending as demonstrated by the verses below:

> *Then He appointed twelve, that they might be with Him and **that He might** send **them out** to preach, and **to have power to heal** sicknesses and to cast out demons. (Mark 3:14-15, NKJV).*

> *And He called the twelve to Himself, and **began to send them out** two by two, and gave them **power over unclean spirits**. (Mark 6:7, NKJV).*

2.2. Authorized through healing miracles

There is undeniably no better way to explain how God authorizes us through healing than demonstrating his power at work through testimonials.

> *People of Israel, listen! God **publicly endorsed** Jesus the Nazarene by doing powerful miracles, wonders, and signs through him, as you well know. (Acts 2:22, NLT).*

A) *Healings in the Koinonia church*
Sunday service, April 1999, La Paz, Bolivia.

After preaching, I was asked with insistence to measure the legs of several individuals before praying for shorts legs to be healed. Of course, I also prayed for other needs. Some short legs seemed to grow out to the same length as the other legs. This worked as a point of contact for the faith of many as several people then testified that they were healed of different health conditions. One man, in particular, said that he was instantly healed of a chronicle condition and pain. Others testified that God had touched their spine, back or neck aches, etc. Pastor Angel, the senior pastor of the church, had not been able to bow down and sit with his knees bowed. One day after he had been ministered to during this service, he visited a friend. As he took a look at his friend's books, he suddenly realized that he was bowing down, sitting with his knees bowed without any pain or difficulty. Later, he testified that he had not been able to do this for several years.

Only a few of those who were touched by God for their healing gave testimonies then even though many other people were touched by God for healing through the great manifestation of His power during that service.

This enables us to say that, as Christ Himself was authorized by the Father, so were the apostles Peter and John authorized by Christ, the Son. And indeed, the chief priests recognized that the apostles Peter and John had authority:

> *And they set the men in their midst and repeatedly demanded, By what sort of power or by what kind of authority did [such people as] you do this [healing]? (Acts 4:7, AMP).*

The Greek word for apostle, *'apostello'*, means 'a sent one'. Consequently, they were the ones that are 'SENT by God', which means that they were the special authorized ones.

When the Gospel was taken to new geographical territories, as the apostles crossed the borderlines to other countries, the kingdom of God was established where they were. Similarly, when the churches were planted in new areas, as we see in the Book of Acts, it was done through the apostles. Therefore, the breakthrough of the Gospel and divine success in church growth are not based on church growth techniques or human methods. They are not based on business-building principles or marketing psychology. In huge parts of the body of Christ, this has become a substitution for the real thing, namely divine authority based mandate and apostolic authority. So, if divine authorization and mandate are lacking, victory will be absent and we shall fail utterly. This can be described as nothing less than a satanic betrayal.

As previously mentioned, the word 'apostle' means 'a sent one.' The Holy Spirit *sent* Paul and Barnabas. This way they were directly authorized by the Holy Spirit Himself:

> *As they ministered to the Lord and fasted, the Holy Spirit said, 'Now separate to Me Barnabas and Saul for the work to which I have called them.' Then, having fasted, prayed, and laid hands on them, they sent them away. So, being sent out by the Holy Spirit, they went.*

(Acts 13:2-4b, NKJV).

Let's consider other instances of healings to consolidate the importance of the need to be sent to carry the divine mandate and operate under authorization.

B) Healing of a shoe-shine boy
December 2001, El Prado, La Paz.

Between Christmas and New Year's celebration, I had a walk in La Paz' town center on the El Prado Street. I was on my way to a Chinese restaurant. As I was walking along the main street, two shoe-shine boys came towards me. They showed me there was something wrong with the eyes of one of them. I laid my hands on the boy's eyes and prayed for him in the name of Jesus Christ. He thanked me and I pointed up towards heaven and went away.

After a week or so, I met them again. They walked towards me happily pointing to the boy's eyes. His eyes looked perfect, and they eagerly told me that he was healed after I had prayed for him. They said 'thank you sir', but I pointed up towards heaven and said 'Thank you to God'.

C) Healings taking place
Wimbledon YMCA summer 2006

After sharing the pulpit with fellow minister in the Lord, Mrs. Marianne Eidsvik, We started ministering to the people with prayer and laying on of hands. A woman came forward and said she had a terrible pain in her leg. I measured the length of her legs and told her to watch. One of her legs looked slightly shorter than the other. I prayed, and the shorter leg moved to the same length as the other, as she watched. Then we prayed for a lump in her breast.

Some days after, we got a text message from somebody as regards this woman saying that a healing had taken place. We got in contact and several weeks later she came to the church with us. She told with joy that when she had come back to the doctor and had a new check, there was no lump in her breast anymore. And the pain in her leg was completely gone. Also, other people that were ministered to at that event testified about healing.

D) Example of instant healing miracle
Kairos Church, Sunday, January 21, 2001, La Paz, Bolivia.

As I finished preaching, I invited people forward to be ministered to. As soon as I started ministering, one after the other was healed. We tested people before and after we prayed for them.

I also prayed corporately for people in the congregation that had not come forward. Many observed instant healings that were taking place and the prayer line became bigger.

I was about to test one lady's hearing after prayer, but she shouted 'No... no... I can hear, I know I am healed, it is not necessary to check it'. I was still able to test it so that the others that needed healing could see it. This was very important, because if we don't get the testimonies and demonstrations there and then, it can limit the amount of healing miracles that could take place.

When the people saw the demonstration of the lady's healing, many others had faith for instant healing too. We tested many people on the platform and demonstrated to the congregation that several people had been instantly healed. Lots of clear-cut, instant-healing miracles happened before the service was over. People with different health issues including spine and back problems received healing. I continued to minister for several hours and more people with hearing problems and deafness were also healed.

E) Other healing miracles
Asambleas de Dios Church, Sunday 28 January 2001, El Alto, Los Andes

My preaching lasted for quite a while before I started to minister to the people. Many of them came forward. One healing took place after the other. Especially, various hearing impairments were healed. Many people testified and demonstrated that they were healed of spine and back problems, etc. I also prayed corporately for people in the congregation that had not come forward. Many people with back, spine and neck problems testified about and demonstrated their healing. After I had prayed for the people in the congregation for the healing of eye conditions, many came forward and testified about their instant healing.

One woman had a stiff knee, which was clearly visible by all. As I prayed for the congregation corporately, I gave commandments in the name of Jesus: 'You that could not see, see. You that could not hear, hear. You who could not jump, jump now. You who could not bow your legs, bow them in the name of Jesus. Do what you could not do before in the name of Jesus'. This woman received those words and bowed her stiff knee. After a while, she came forward to the platform and demonstrated with moves on her knee for everybody to see. She could bow her knee freely and walk home from that service with both her legs functioning properly.

F) Instant healing from blind eye
Vida Nueva Church, October 2003, El Alto.

After preaching, I prayed for the people in the congregation corporately. I told the people who were deaf in one ear or with hearing issues to put their hand on the ear that needed healing. I also insisted on people with eye or sight problems to do the same. Then we asked people that were instantly healed to come forward and give their testimony. Three women came forward. They all testified that their hearing was healed. Two of them testified that they got their hearing back on one of their ears. Owing to the translation, it was unclear whether the third one got back her hearing or was healed from reduced hearing. But she definitively gave a clear testimony that her hearing was healed on one ear.

Then there was a short lady that came up on the platform. She stood on my left. She was pointing to her blind eye all the time. As the service was about to end and the people moved around, I took her down from the platform and we stood in front of the meeting hall nearby the pulpit. Together with Robert, my interpreter, we instructed the woman to repeat all I did with my fingers and hand. Then we blocked the good eye. She could not repeat anything. Then I laid my hand on the eye and commanded it to be healed in the name of Jesus Christ. We checked again. When I lifted one finger, she lifted one. When I lifted two, she did the same. I waved my hand and she did the same. Her blind eye was healed. Praise and glory to God!

G) Hearing healed on both ears
San Buenaventura, 2003, Beni river, Bolivia

One evening I am ministering in Filadelfia church in a quiet town by the Beni River bank. There are very few people present this evening. A woman comes to me to be prayed for. She says that because of the condition of her hearing she is not even able to listen to the radio or to have normal conversations with people. As I pray for her I almost get furious in my spirit because of the spiritual resistance against instant healing manifestations that we have experienced so far since our arrival at the lowlands. Spontaneously, I put my thumbs firmly on her ears, and I shout 'in the name of Jesus Christ be healed and hear properly'. I remove my thumbs as fast as quickly as possible, as to remove any vacuum in the ears. I have no idea why I spontaneously did this when I was under the anointing.

The meeting is soon ended and people start going home. The following day another meeting was planned at the same place. There are very few people present. As I am preaching, a truck stops outside the church. The truck is full of people. They all come into the service and fill up the church. Then as we finish preaching, the women we prayed for the day before to get her hearing restored on both ears comes forward and gives her testimony. She was healed. I think I understand why this truckload of people suddenly came to the church. They must have heard about this woman's healing. Now she tells us that she can listen to the radio when she is alone in her house and she can chat with people again. She is so happy and excited! We test her hearing and she can hear what we are saying perfectly well. We continue ministering to people with laying on of hands. Before the service is over, several people lay on the floor, under the power of God, praising Him.

H) *Saved and restored*
Reyes, Asambleas de Dios, Bolivia 2003

The meeting was going to be over two evenings. The first evening, after preaching, we invited people to receive salvation and restoration with God:
Several backslidden people come back to God and are renewed in their relationship with Him. One family comes forward and they give their life to Christ for the first time.

The following evening, several more come back to God and get their relationship with God renewed. In addition, a whole bunch of teenagers comes forward and they give their life to Christ for the first time. No instant healing manifestations, but a great victory anyway.

Both evenings, I was preaching with power about the Law and Commandments of God, God's judgment and the wages of sin... about being ready if we should die now or if the church should be raptured in this moment. By the power of the Holy Spirit, the preaching was aiming at the conscience of people as strong and effective as possible. Then I preached with the same power and strength about God's grace, the atonement, and about complete forgiveness and total restoration through the blood of Jesus.

I)Healed by the power of God
Asambleas de Dios Church Cochabamba, Bolivia 2003.

I was the main speaker in an almost weeklong campaign. Several people testified about their healing.

I remember a young girl in particular who came forward along with her mother. She had long, dark hair. They told me she was deaf in one ear. I could see that the deaf ear was bent. We blocked the good ear as we instructed her to repeat what I was saying. She could not repeat or hear anything I was saying. Then I prayed and commanded the ear to be healed in the name of Jesus Christ. We repeated the same procedure. Now she could hear and repeat everything I said. The ear was still bent but her hearing was healed to the glory of God! In addition, another young girl could not hear on one ear. After we prayed for her she could hear on it.

K) Healing of an almost totally blind girl
Branch of Vida Nueva Church, La Paz

A mother came with a little girl who was totally losing her sight in both eyes. The girl was crying without ceasing. I tried to get her to look at me because I wanted to check how blind she was… if she could see anything at all. But when I tried to draw her attention to me, she cried and answered back in despair, 'I can't, I can't see!' She kept crying because her sight was damaged. I prayed for her. I commanded the eyes to be healed in the name of Jesus Christ. We waited a little while. Later on, we asked the people who had been prayed for to testify. The mother of this girl came forward, looking excited and happy and crying of joy. She told us that the girl could see. We tested the girl and she could repeat all the movements I did with my hand and fingers. She could see! She was healed to the glory of God.

A woman of the Aymará people also testified of the healing of her shoulders, arms and legs. Another woman who spoke only the Quechua language also testified through an interpreter that she got her hearing back in one ear. She also gave her life to Jesus even though she probably did not understand a word of what I was saying.

L) Instant healing miracles
Congregación Cristiana La Paz, 10 January, 2001,
Los Andes.

I was preaching about authorization in the name of Jesus Christ. As I had ended my preaching, an elderly man lifted up his hand. He told me that he was deaf in one ear and asked if I could pray for his healing. He came forward to the pulpit. We asked him to repeat what I was saying. Then we blocked his good ear. He could not repeat anything I was saying even when I was very close to him. I then laid my hands on his ear and commanded it to be healed in the name of Jesus Christ.

We tested again, and now he could repeat everything that I said. The man was healed. I would say he was probably about ninety percentage healed instantly.

Then his son came forward. He was wearing thick glasses and could not see anything on one of his eyes. We instructed him to copy the movements I was doing with my hand and my fingers. We blocked the eye that could see. I went as close up as possible. I lifted one finger, two fingers, waved my hands. No reaction. He could not see anything. Then I laid my hands on the blind eye and commanded it to be healed in the name of Jesus Christ. We tested again. We blocked the eye that he had been able to see with all the time. I held one finger up as close as possible to the eye that had been blind. I lifted one finger. He lifted one. I lifted two fingers. He did the same. I waved my hand and he did the same. I even went to the other end of the platform and he could repeat all the movements I did with my hands. He was healed.

This was the first time in my life I had experienced such instant healings. We even took people on the platform before they were healed so everybody could see. Then we ministered to them in the name of Jesus, and they were instantly healed there and then.

2.3. Authorized by calling

Remember the consecration of the priests in The Old Testament. It was forbidden to let the anointing oil come on a layman's body. It was only available for the priests. In other words, it was only for those in the ministry. It was, therefore, a matter of authorization. Authority follows the call to ministry.

What does it mean to be 'authorized by *calling?*' It means to be authorized according to *predestination* and *election*. For instance, God has chosen Israel. The same way, He has chosen the Church. And He has chosen certain people for certain ministries and offices.

An excellent book on the topic of election and grace is the book *The Destiny of Israel and the Church* by Derek Prince. In particular, chapters 8 and 18 that are respectively entitled "Election" and

"Election and the Church", give excellent explanations on this topic.

The point here is that, if someone is chosen or elected 'from mother's womb' or before 'being born', it is obviously by grace:

> *For the children not yet being born, nor having done any good or evil, that the purpose of God according to **election** might stand, not of works but of Him who calls. So then it is not of him who wills, nor of him who runs, but of God who shows mercy. (Romans 9:11-16, NKJV).*

Election is here contrary to human effort; it is contrary to 'willing' or 'running'. For that reason, election and predestination equal grace. It is actually called 'the election of grace':

> *Even so then, at this present time there is a remnant according to the **election of grace**. (Romans 11:5, NKJV).*

Then again, election and grace are in contrast to 'works', that means in contrast to human effort:

> *And if by grace, then it is no longer by works; if it were, grace would no longer be grace. (Romans 11:6, NIV).*

Now, make note of the two following expressions:

1. *The **election of** grace. (Romans 11:5 NKJV).*
2. *According to election **might stand, not of works but of** Him **who** calls. (Romans 9:11 NKJV).*

The emphasis here is, **'election... of Him who *calls*'**, which means that the same way election is related to grace, it is related to 'calling' or 'being called'.

2.4. Authorized by grace

According to the principle of election and predestination, Paul was called. Be aware of the way 'called' and 'grace' are inter-related (interwoven):

> *But when it pleased God, who separated me from my mother's womb and **called** me through His **grace**. (Galatians 1:15, NKJV).*

> *...to reveal his Son in me so that I might preach him among the Gentiles, my immediate response was not to consult any human being. (Galatians 1:16, NIV).*

This also shows us that one cannot choose to be an apostle. Only those who are predestined and elected by God can have that office or ministry. Paul had a clear-cut and concise call to the ministry and office of an apostle:

> *Paul, a bondservant of Jesus Christ, called to be an apostle, separated to the gospel of God. (Romans 1:1, NKJV).*

The same principle of being *chosen* through *grace* applies for the ministry and office of a prophet:

> *Before I formed you in the womb I knew you; Before you were born I sanctified you; I ordained you a prophet to the nations. (Jeremiah 1:5, NKJV).*

A prophet is then called and chosen according to God's predestination and election. That means that the prophet is chosen and called by grace. The following Bible passage does not talk about election and calling to ministry in particular, but the principle we find here is exactly the same: to be called requires predestination! Those God "foreknew", are the ones that are predestined, that means that they are chosen or elected:

> *For whom He foreknew, He also* **predestined** *to be conformed to the image of His Son, that He might be the firstborn among many brethren. Moreover* **whom He predestined,** ***these He also*** **called***; whom He called, these He also justified; and whom He justified, these He also glorified. (Romans 8:29-31, NKJV).*

We are indeed authorized through grace. On the one hand, this authority is not obtained by human efforts and self-improvement. It is not given as a reward for walking in the Spirit, righteous living, praying, fasting or endurance in spiritual warfare. We don't receive authorization as a consequence of sanctification either. On the other hand, if we do not walk in the Spirit, but walk in the flesh, this divine authority that is given will not have its free and unhindered flow through us. And of course, the lack of prayer and confession of the Word of God will also dramatically restrict its flow. As much as true prayer and fasting will increase and strengthen the effect of this authority, the lack of sanctification will put breaks to its manifestation.

True spiritual warfare goes along with the way we exercise this authority, based on the victory of Christ. In true spiritual warfare, we never wrestle to *obtain* authority and victory. Instead, we wrestle from a *position* of authority because the victory has already been obtained for us by Christ. We are already placed in a position of victory and authority in Christ. The main dilemma here is the lack of revelation, the lack of knowledge. Because of such lacks concerning these facts, people try to obtain what is already theirs in Christ. This is a big problem. As these facts become clear to us, it is our responsibility to start walking in the light of these biblical facts, act accordingly and stand firm on them even when the circumstances seem to tell us that these facts can't be true. As we do this, we will gradually manifest this victory and position of authority. Yes, the manifestation of the authority and victory of Christ through us is a result of revelation.

2.5. Authorized through anointing

To anoint (or to be anointed) is a legal matter. 'Authority' is very much a legal expression. Let us now look at the connection between anointing and authorization knowing that the Holy Spirit and power are interrelated (connected). Because the anointing represents God's authorization, *the anointing* is *with the Holy Spirit* and *with power.* Therefore, we must state that authority is a condition for power. The power is a consequence of the authority.

The example of Saul:

*The Lord forbid that I should do this to my lord the king
and attack the Lord's anointed one, for the Lord himself
has chosen him. (1 Samuel 24:6b, NLT).*

*Behold, your eyes have seen how the Lord gave you today
into my hands in the cave. Some told me to kill you, but I
spared you; I said, I will not put forth my hand against my
lord, for he is the Lord's anointed.
(1 Samuel 24:10, AMP).*

This passage refers to when David and King Saul were in conflict. David could have killed Saul but he did not do it because he acknowledged that, as Saul had been authorized by the Lord, he was still the Lord's anointed. Nevertheless, the Spirit of the Lord had actually left Saul at this stage:

*The Spirit of the Lord had left Saul. And an evil spirit that
was sent by the Lord terrified him.
(1 Samuel 16:14, NIRV).*

*And the Spirit of Jehovah turned aside from Saul, and a
spirit of sadness from Jehovah terrified him.
(1 Samuel 16:14, YLT).*

The fact that Saul still was the Lord's anointed after the Spirit of the Lord had left him shows us that anointing is a legal matter. In our context, we do not have a human court or human law in mind to sort out things, but the principle is the same.

When Saul was anointed with the anointing oil, God thereby authorized him. How could he still hold this authority (that is: how could he still be the Lord's anointed), after the Spirit of the Lord had left him? The answer is indicated below:

Let's clarify this:

Cause: the gifts and calling of God are irrevocable [this is the principle].

Effect: God does not change His mind or take away the gifts He has given to those He has chosen [see Romans 11:29 above].

CHAPTER III
ANOINTING: A LIFE-LONG AUTHORIZATION

3.1. God's authorization lasts for life

> *No one who performs a miracle in my name will soon be able to speak evil of me. (Mark 9:39, NLT).*

When God gives someone authority, it lasts for life. It does not come and go according to variation in spiritual condition:

> *Not everyone who says to me, 'Lord, Lord,' will enter the kingdom of heaven. Only those who do what my Father in heaven wants will enter. Many will say to me on that day, 'Lord! Lord! Didn't we prophesy in your name? Didn't we drive out demons in your name? Didn't we do many miracles in your name?' Then I will tell them clearly, *'I never knew you. Get away from me, you who **do evil!' (Matthew 7:21-23, NIRV).*

*"I never knew you." He, Jesus, was there because the miracles were real and performed in His name and by His power. Thus, we in some way could say that 'he knew them'. He was there, so they probably believed that he 'knew them' and recognized them. It was the name of Jesus that produced the miracles, not the people using the name. It turned out that he had not acknowledged their motives. Hence, Jesus now says, 'I never knew you'. He did not recognize them in this context. That is why they lost their reward,

which is very much related to the kingdom of God and the rule of Christ within the period of thousand years (see Revelation 2:26). For explanatory purposes, we will quote from Matthew 7:21-23 once again: "…Didn't we prophesy in your name? Didn't we drive out demons in your name? Didn't we do many miracles in your name?' Then I will tell them clearly, 'I never knew you. Get away from me, you who do evil!" Be aware of the following in this Bible verse:

1. What they did, was to prophesy, to cast out demons and do many miracles, actually in Jesus' name.

2. To do these things is definitively not evil, but rather good.

3. Why is Jesus then saying to them, "Get away from me, you who do evil"?

4. Jesus is therefore not referring to operating in His name in prophesy, casting out demons and performing miracles when He calls it 'do evil'.

5. What He is referring to is the motives in their hearts when doing these things.

6. What they were doing was not motivated by or a result of the new, divine nature in their born again spirits. On the one hand, what is a result of the divine nature in us is what is begotten (born) of God. This, we compare with gold, which can never burn, but will always survive the fire. On the other hand, that which is not begotten (born) of God, is those things that originate from our own natural man and not in God, namely the things stemming from our own old nature. Those are the things called evil ('you who do evil'). These latter things can be compared to hay, straw and wood, etc., the kind of materials

that cannot survive the fire. This means that regardless of the number of people saved and the many miracles performed through any of our actions and works, we may lose our reward, in particular, some of our reward in the Millennium (the soon coming thousand yearlong rule of Christ here on earth):

> *For no one can lay any foundation other than the one already laid, which is Jesus Christ. If anyone builds on this foundation using gold, silver, costly stones, wood, hay or straw, their work will be shown for what it is, because the Day will bring it to light. It will be revealed with fire, and the fire will test the quality of each person's work. If what has been built survives, the builder will receive a reward. If it is burned up, the builder will suffer loss but yet will be saved – even though only as one escaping through the flames. (1 Corinthians 3:11-15 NIV).*

At present, the Kingdom is in heaven. Jesus will come and reign on this earth for thousand years. Then the Kingdom will be fully manifested on this earth. In the meantime, the Kingdom is temporarily demonstrated here on earth by the Church as she takes new territory for the sake of the Gospel.

It is also important to note that not all believers will be given power over the nations and rule them with a rod of iron. Only the overcoming believers will do so:

> *And he that overcomes, and keeps my works to the end, to him will I give power over the nations. And he shall rule them with a rod of iron; as the vessels of a potter shall they be broken to shivers: even as I received of my Father. (Revelation 2:26-27, AKJV).*

This is therefore not a question of salvation at all, but a question of wages and rewards related to stewardship.

These people operated in the name of Jesus: no one can drive out demons and do miracles in the name of Jesus without having the authority to do so. These people were not of the devil, but their spiritual condition was wrong. And, despite this condition, remember what Jesus Himself said:

*Now John answered and said, 'Master, we saw someone
casting out demons in Your name, and we forbade him
because he does not follow with us.' But Jesus said to him,
'Do not forbid him, for he who is not against us is on our
side.' (Luke 9:49-50, NKJV).*

*Now John answered Him, saying, 'Teacher, we saw
someone who does not follow us casting out demons in
Your name, and we forbade him because he does not
follow us.' But Jesus said, 'Do not forbid him, for no one
who works a miracle in My name can soon afterward
speak evil of Me.' (Mark 9:38-39, NKJV).*

*And though I have the gift of prophecy, and understand
all mysteries and all knowledge, and though I have all
faith, so that I could remove mountains, but have not love,
I am nothing. (1 Corinthians 13:2, NKJV).*

This last Bible verse indicates that these gifts are irrevocable. Even when the spiritual condition of an individual sinks to a low or to a zero level so to speak, the gifts of prophecy, knowledge and miracles may still be at work.   Also, through periods of many years, our spiritual condition may vary. As far as our motives, these may vary through the years depending on our spiritual condition. The same is true concerning what has its origin in, and is born of the Spirit versus what is born of the flesh or the soul (our natural man). It is also possible that things are begotten by God (can be considered as precious metals that can stand the fire), whilst we continue in the flesh (can be considered as hay, straw and wood, which are substances that are not capable of surviving the fire):

> *Are you so foolish? After beginning by means of the Spirit, are you now trying to finish by means of the flesh? (Galatians 3:3, NIV).*

3.2. The priests were authorized through the anointing

The priests were anointed for ministry and office as a part of their consecration:

> *Clothe your brother, Aaron, and his sons with these garments, and* **then *anoint* and ordain them.** *Consecrate them so they can serve as my priests. (Exodus 28:41, NLT).*

Only those who were chosen for the office and ministry of a priest could be anointed with this oil:

> *It shall not be poured upon a layman's body, nor shall you make any other like it in composition; it is holy, and you shall hold it sacred. (Exodus 30:32, AMP).*

The anointing oil shall not be poured upon a layman's body! Other people did not have the authority to operate in the ministry of a priest: they were not authorized through the anointing oil. Therefore, the act of anointing with oil represents authorization. Receiving the anointing oil involves the act of consecration. The anointing is for ministry work. The anointing follows the ministry.

The Holy Spirit calls people to particular spiritual work. We are authorized within the realms of the work or tasks to which we are called. We are called to a specific ministry or office and thereby anointed and authorized for this particular ministry or office.

In Ephesians, we find five New Testament ministries:

Now these are the gifts Christ gave to the church: the apostles, the prophets, the evangelists, and the pastors and teachers. (Ephesians 4:11, NLT).

These five ministries are at least authorized by the Scripture, based on Ephesians 4:11. Furthermore, Jesus, the Son of Man, was Himself authorized for His earthly ministry through the anointing oil of the Holy Spirit:

How God anointed Jesus of Nazareth with the Holy Spirit and with power, who went about doing good and healing all who were oppressed by the devil, for God was with Him. (Acts 10:38, NKJV).

We could say, 'God authorized Jesus with the Holy Spirit and with power'. The above-mentioned event took place when John the Baptist baptized Jesus in the river Jordan, and the Holy Spirit came down on Jesus like a dove. Jesus was anointed for His earthly ministry (Matthew 3:16).

Here is a parallel Bible passage, describing Jesus' authorization through the anointing more in details:

And He was handed the book of the prophet Isaiah. And when He had opened the book, He found the place where it was written: "The Spirit of the Lord is upon Me, Because **He has *anointed*** Me *To preach the gospel to the poor; He has sent Me to heal the broken-hearted, to proclaim liberty to the captives And recovery of sight to the blind, to set at liberty those who are oppressed."*
(Luke 4:17-18, NKJV).

3.3. Example of an authority-based ministry

God, the Father, authorized Jesus:

God the Father has authorized and certified Him and put His seal of endorsement upon Him. (John 6:27b, AMP).

The earthly ministry of Jesus was authority-based:

And it came to pass, when Jesus ended these words, the multitudes were astonished at his teaching, for he was teaching them **as *having authority***, *and not as the scribes.*
(Matthew 7:28-29 YLT).

When we preach, do we sound like the scribes, as people without any authority? How would that sound? Or do we sound like Jesus? That is, as people with authority. How would that sound? If we do not preach with the same authority, how can we expect the same or similar results? Are we teaching as people not having authority? How ought we to speak the Word of God? Obviously, according to the Word of God, we ought to speak with boldness:

> *And for me, that utterance may be given to me, that I may open my mouth boldly, to make known the mystery of the gospel, For which I am an ambassador in bonds: that therein I may speak boldly, as I ought to speak.*
> *(Ephesians 6:19-20).*

This will sound as someone having authority! And this is how we must preach to activate the anointing!

> *Then they were all amazed, so that they questioned among themselves, saying, 'What is this? What new doctrine is this? For with authority He commands even the unclean spirits, and they obey Him.' (Mark 1:27, NKJV).*

> *Jesus knew right away what they were thinking, and said, "Why are you so skeptical? Which is simpler: to say to the paraplegic, 'I forgive your sins,' or say, 'Get up, take your stretcher, and start walking'? Well, just so it's clear that I'm the Son of Man and* **authorized** *to do* **either, or both...** *" (He looked now at the paraplegic), 'Get up. Pick up your stretcher and go home.' And the man did it – got up, grabbed his stretcher, and walked out, with everyone there watching him. They rubbed their eyes, incredulous – and then praised God, saying, 'We've never seen anything like this!' (Mark 2:8-12, MSG).*

Jesus was authorized by the Father to bring (the message of) forgiveness as well as to bring healing. How much more would divine authorization be required for us before we could be used for such a purpose? Indeed, to bring God's forgiveness and the healing of the sick requires authorization.

3.4. Operating with divine authority

The key to understanding how to operate with divine authority is found in the expression: 'in the name', 'in His name' and 'in my name', etc.

1. We are authorized through the name of Jesus.
2. We are authorized by the anointing to use the name of Jesus as well as to operate in His name.

3.5. Power of attorney

The power of attorney actually means that there is a written authorization. In fact, everyone who participates in the New Covenant also participates in its written promises, its inheritance, its covenantal rights and privileges. A power of attorney is a document that gives one party authority to act on another party's behalf. It is an authorization to act on someone else's behalf. There must be a minimum of two parties involved: the authorizer and the one that is authorized. In our case, Christ Jesus is the authorizer and we are the party that is authorized. This is how this principle works:

- Peter said to the crippled man: "In the name of Jesus Christ of Nazareth, stand up and walk." (Acts 3:5-7).
- Paul said to the evil spirit: "In the name of Jesus Christ, Come out of her!" (Acts 16:17-19).

The name of Jesus Christ was like a signature they used. This signature, the name of Jesus Christ, is legally valid. Now, the declarations of the apostles were like a legally valid document, stamped with the name and seal of Jesus Christ. Or we could say, that the Word of God, its facts and promises, which they acted upon when they spoke, were the written, legal document, and the signature and seal was the name of Jesus. Their actions were authorized through the use of that name.

The name of Jesus is indeed like a signet ring, used as a stamp on a seal while the actual signature is stamped on the seal. In the book of Esther, we find the expression, "sealed with the king's signet ring" (Esther 3:12). Besides, in Esther 8:8b we read: "for whatever is written in the king's name and sealed with the king's signet ring no one can revoke." Yes, this could truly be said about the name of the *King* Jesus Christ. And we are entrusted with the name of Jesus. We can use it like a legal valid stamp. We 'stamp' our prayers with the name of Jesus like a legal, valid signature. We are entrusted with that name. Go ahead and use it. Take advantage of it now! When we are confronted with the enemy and we approach him, we find the same principle is in operation.

Whatever is 'written' in Christ's name and sealed with His name, no one can revoke. And we are given this signet ring. He has entrusted us with it. And He is not the one that uses it. We are the ones using His signet ring now.

In fact, the name of Jesus has authorized us to approach God, the Father representatively, on Christ's behalf:

> *And when that time comes, you will ask nothing of Me [you will need to ask Me no questions]. I assure you, most solemnly I tell you, that My Father will grant you whatever you ask in My Name [as presenting all that I AM]. Up to this time you have not asked a [single] thing in My Name [as presenting all that I AM]; but now ask and keep on asking and you will receive, so that your joy (gladness, delight) may be full and complete ... At that time you will ask (pray) in My Name; and I am not saying that I will ask the Father on your behalf [for it will be unnecessary]. For the Father Himself [tenderly] loves you because you have loved Me and have believed that I came out from the Father. (John 16:23-24, 26-27, AMP).*

Notice verse 23 says that "My Father will grant you whatever you ask in My name." Compare this with verse 26 and 27 where it says "**I am *not* saying that I will ask the Father on your behalf** [for it will not be necessary] for the Father Himself [tenderly] loves you."

This is an extraordinary statement! What Jesus is saying is that *'you can go directly to the Father now'*; *'you don't need to come to me and ask me to go to the Father on your behalf [because you (think you) are unworthy to approach the Father on your own']*. He is saying, *'you can go to the Father yourself now'*. That is, *'when you come to the Father in My Name'*. This is because His name represents all that Jesus is.

Of course, we do not have 'authority' towards the Father. But authority in our context means, 'legal right'. As we already have mentioned, it is about the power of attorney.

Through the name of Jesus, we have the 'legal right' to come before the Father. We hold the Power of Attorney to come before the Father directly when we approach Him in the name of Jesus Christ. So, we may paraphrase it as follows: *'I assure you, most solemnly I tell you, that My Father will grant you whatever you ask representatively, on my behalf, based on The Power of Attorney, sealed and signed with My name.'* Or *'Up to this time you have not asked a [single] thing, representatively, on my behalf, based on this Power of Attorney. At that time, you will ask (pray) representatively, on my behalf, based on this Power of Attorney.'*

3.6. Our legal basis: Justification

We had all sinned and, of course, had no legal right to come before God, the Father. Neither did we have any legal right to contact, communion and fellowship with Him: the Bible says all have sinned and come short of the glory of God and the wages of sin is death. So, according to universal justice, sin has to be punished. If sin is not punished it is unjust, it is unrighteous. But God, in His great wisdom, managed to justify us, and at the same time, punish all our sins and thereby continue to be just. Let us take a brief, closer look at this:

> *Being justified freely by His grace through the redemption that is in Christ Jesus, whom God set forth as a propitiation by His blood, through faith, to demonstrate His righteousness, because in His forbearance God had passed over the sins that were previously committed, to demonstrate at the present time His righteousness, that He might be just and the justifier of the one who has faith in Jesus. (Romans 3:24-27, NKJV).*

By letting the punishment fall on Jesus, He 'demonstrates at the present time His righteousness'. And because He let our punishment fall on Jesus, He could justify us from our sins, and at the same time still be righteous. 'Justified' is a legal term. We were justified because justice was exercised through Jesus being *judged* to death because of our sins. As a consequence, we can say that we have a legal right to come before the Father in the name of Jesus.

3.7. Justified through the covenant of the blood of Jesus

Much more then, having now been justified by His blood,
we shall be saved from wrath through Him.
(Romans 5:9, NKJV).

Indeed, through the blood of Jesus we have a legal right to approach the Father directly in the name of Jesus:

Therefore, brethren, having boldness to enter the Holiest
by the blood of Jesus (19), let us draw near.
(Hebrews 10:19, 22a, NKJV).

This leads us to conclude that we are also authorized through covenant too: God has made a covenant with man. God is not unjust or unrighteous. God is both just and righteous. Therefore, we can be sure that God will keep the covenant with its promises:

Resting on the faithfulness of Christ our Lord,
Resting on the fullness of His own sure word,
Resting on His wisdom, on His love and pow'r,
Resting on His *covenant* from 'hour to 'hour.[1]

For this is My blood of the new covenant, which is shed
for many for the remission of sins.
(Matthew 26:28, NKJV).

---

[1] Hymn by Frances Ridley Havergal (1836 – 1879), in Watchman Nee, The Better Covenant (New York: Christian Fellowship Publishers, 1982, 9.

This Bible verse shows us that there is a covenant in the blood of Jesus. Further on, it shows that the blood of the covenant represents the remission of sins. Therefore, the covenant is based on grace and not on "our own power or godliness" (Acts 3:12, NKJV).

A covenant is a formal agreement between at least two parties. This covenant is guaranteed and 'sealed' by the blood of Jesus. Besides, it is established on better promises than the first covenant (Hebrews 8:6).

Chapter IV
WHAT IS THE CHURCH ENTRUSTED WITH?

4.1. Jesus has entrusted the Church

The church is 'given' the name of Jesus. When we give something to someone, we entrust them with that gift. Jesus' name is 'given among men', which means that we are entrusted with His name:

> *Neither is there salvation in any other: for there is none other name under heaven given among men, whereby we must be saved. (Acts 4:12).*

4.1.1. Entrusted to command the brethren

The church is entrusted with the right to operate in the name of Jesus in commanding the brothers and sisters. Certainly, we may 'command' the 'brethren' representatively on Christ's behalf, in His stead, in His power and on His authority. Nevertheless, we must be careful not to do so in our own name:

> *Now we command you, brethren, in the name of our Lord Jesus Christ, that ye withdraw yourselves from every brother that walks disorderly, and not after the tradition which he received of us. (2 Thessalonians 3:6, KJV).*

His name represents His authority:

*Now we charge you, brethren, in the **name** and on the **authority** of our Lord Jesus Christ (the Messiah) that you withdraw and keep away from every brother (fellow believer) who is slack in the performance of duty and is disorderly, living as a shirker and not walking in accord with the traditions and instructions that you have received from us. (2 Thessalonians 3:6, AMP).*

4.1.2. Entrusted to bring thanksgiving

We are entrusted with the right to operate in the name of Jesus before the Father in bringing thanksgiving. When we come before the Father, bringing our thanksgivings, we must come to Him and express our thanksgivings representatively on Christ's behalf, in His stead, in His power, and on His authority:

Giving thanks always for all things unto God and the Father in the name of our Lord Jesus Christ. (Ephesians 5:20, KJV).

4.1.3. Entrusted in our words and deeds

We are entrusted with the right to operate in the name of Jesus in our words and deeds. Our words, be it preaching, teaching, counseling and so on, must be done representatively, on Christ's behalf, in His stead, by His power and on His authority. The same goes for our 'deeds' (our acts, works, actions and all kinds of spiritual work) must be done representatively on Christ's behalf, in His stead, by His power and on His authority:

*And whatsoever ye do in word or deed, do all in the name
of the Lord Jesus, giving thanks to God and the Father by
him. (Colossians 3:17).*

4.1.4. Entrusted to speak and teach the Word of God

We are entrusted with the right to operate in the name of Jesus
when we speak and teach the Word of God. We must speak and
teach representatively on Christ's behalf, in His stead, in His
power and on His authority.

*So they sent for them, and commanded them not to speak
[as His representatives] or teach at all in the name of
Jesus [using Him as their authority]. (Acts 4:18, AMP).*

4.1.5. Entrusted to preach the Word of God

We are entrusted with the right to operate in the name of Jesus
when we preach and it makes a huge difference: this will cause us
to preach with boldness. Our preaching must be done
representatively on Christ's behalf, in His stead, in His power and
on His authority (and not on our own):

*But Barnabas took him, and brought him to the apostles,
and declared unto them how he had seen the Lord in the
way, and that he had spoken to him, and how he had
preached boldly at Damascus in the name of Jesus.
(Acts 9:27, KJV).*

4.1.6. Entrusted for discussions based on the Word

We are entrusted with the right to operate in the name of Jesus when it comes to speeches and disputes based on God's word. We must speak representatively on Christ's behalf, in His stead, in His power and on His authority:

> *And he spoke boldly in the name of the Lord Jesus, and disputed against the Grecians: but they went about to slay him. (Acts 9:29, KJV).*

4.1.7. Entrusted to anoint the sick with oil

The pastors and elders are entrusted with the right to operate in the name of Jesus, in anointing the sick with oil. We must anoint the sick representatively on Christ's behalf, in his stead, in His power and on His authority:

> *Is any sick among you? Let him call for the elders of the church; and let them pray over him, anointing him with oil in the name of the Lord. (James 5:14, KJV).*

4.1.8. Entrusted to go forth with God's Word

> *Because that for his name's sake they went forth taking nothing of the Gentiles. (3 John 1:7, KJV).*

We are entrusted with the right to operate in the name of Jesus as we go forth with God's Word 'for His name's sake.' This entrustment to go forth in the name of Jesus seems to include financial independence from money that is not given and received in the name of Jesus, as an example if received from non-Christians. This is confirmed by the second part of the Bible verse just quoted above:

> *...went forth taking nothing of the Gentiles.*
> *(3 John 1:7b, KJV).*

When we go forth with God's Word and with the Gospel, we must do it representatively on His behalf, in His stead, in His power, on His authority and not our own.

> *Because that for his name's sake they went forth, taking nothing of the Gentiles. (3 John 1:7, KJV).*

4.1.9. Entrusted to exhort

The church is entrusted with the right to operate in the name of Jesus in exhortation, to exhort, representatively on Christ's behalf, in His stead, in His power and on His authority.

> *Now I exhort you, brethren, by the name of our Lord Jesus Christ, that ye all say the same thing, and that there be not among you divisions; but that ye be perfectly united in the same mind and in the same opinion.*
> *(1 Corinthians 1:10, DARBY).*

In consequence, all exhortation must be done in His name, not in our own.

4.1.10. Entrusted with the name of Jesus

Every believer is entrusted with the name of Jesus and its use:

1. we can use the name of Jesus to approach God in prayer;

2. we can use the name of Jesus when we are confronted with the enemy, for example, to cast out demons.

However, what we, as believers, quite often do wrong when we pray is that we just approach God in prayer and then we expect something to happen. Sometimes, we also wait on God for an answer. To approach God with expectation and waiting on him is of course not wrong. But the problem is that something may be lacking here.

Indeed, most believers know that we have to command evil spirits to come out. We know that asking God to remove the evil spirit is insufficient for a successful result. Nevertheless, what a large number of Christians don't realize is that it works in a similar way when it comes to healing of sickness:

> *And when he had called unto him his twelve disciples, he gave them power against unclean spirits, to cast them out, and to heal all manner of sickness and all manner of disease. (Matthew 10:1, KJV).*

Why should Jesus give *them* power to heal sickness and disease if all that was required was to ask God in prayer and just expecting God to intervene and heal the sick? It would not make any sense, would it? Here is where the church very often has got it wrong. Even our theologians have very often failed us in this matter it seems.

Jesus gave power and authority to the twelve apostles. He gave them 'power over the evil spirits to cast them out'. Most believers will accept that. As an example, we would not say, 'It is not me that cast out the evil spirits, I cannot do that, it is God who does that.' Then we simply turn to God and ask Him to remove the evil spirit from the person that needs deliverance. Most believers would probably not do that. Instead, we would say, 'evil spirit, in the name of Jesus, come out of this person.' But when Jesus gave power and authority to the twelve apostles, it was not only over the evil spirits, He also gave them 'power and authority to cure (heal) diseases.' It wouldn't make any sense if God gave them such power and authority, but they were not supposed to use it, would it?

> *Then he called his twelve disciples together, and gave them power and authority over all devils, and to cure diseases. (Luke 9:1, KJV).*

The apostles did not push the responsibility back to God and leave it there. If we read in the Book of Acts, we will find that they didn't just ask God to heal, and expected something to happen. No, they had to exercise the power and authority that God had given them. And so should we do, if we are going to see similar results today! What we find out from the Bible is that the apostles spoke and gave commandments in the name of Jesus.

Peter said to the crippled man, "what I have I give unto you, in the name of Jesus, stand up and walk." Let's look into the Bible:

> *Then Peter said, Silver and gold have I none; but such as I have give I thee: In the name of Jesus Christ of Nazareth rise up and walk. And he took him by the right hand, and lifted him up: and immediately his feet and anklebones received strength. And he leaping up stood, and walked, and entered with them into the temple, walking, and leaping, and praising God. (Acts 3:6-8, KJV).*

And we are supposed to do the same! Peter was entrusted with the *use* of that name… and he used it when necessary:

> *But Peter said, Silver and gold (money) I do not have; but what I do have, that I give to you: in [the **use** of] the name of Jesus Christ of Nazareth, walk! Then he took hold of the man's right hand with a firm grip and raised him up. And at once his feet and ankle bones became strong and steady, and leaping forth he stood and began to walk, and he went into the temple with them, walking and leaping and praising God. (Acts 3:6-8, AMP).*

Peter did not call for a prayer meeting. He did not stop, seeking guidance. He didn't even ask God to heal the man. The fact is that Peter was fully entrusted with the name of Jesus and its use. God had left it to Peter. He had left the responsibility of the use of that name to Peter. As a result, we see that Peter just gives a command in the name of Jesus. And God is behind him and backs him up.

So, when Peter spoke in the name of Jesus, the power of God was activated and the man was instantly healed.

In another instance, Peter also said, "Jesus Christ heals you." And we are supposed to do the same:

> *And there he found a certain man named Aeneas, which had kept his bed eight years, and was sick of the palsy. And Peter said unto him, Aeneas, Jesus Christ makes you whole: arise, and make thy bed. And he arose immediately. (Acts 9:33-34, KJV).*

Here we see how Peter acts representatively on Christ's behalf. And it is obvious from our text that God backs him up fully. He speaks in Christ's stead. He says, "Jesus Christ makes you whole ('heals you')." Why could Peter say that? How could he know? People mistakenly believe that the main key here is guidance. They think that if we just first find out if Jesus is going to heal this person, then we have got the key to miracles like that. That is a complete misunderstanding and a theological misconception. This doesn't have much to do with guidance. The key here is entrustment: to discover and be aware of the fact that we are entrusted with the name of Jesus and its use; that we are entrusted with God's power; that power is in His name. This fact must be received and acted upon without hesitation. It must be believed and acted upon with the uttermost boldness! Peter acted representatively on Christ's behalf by being bold enough to say,

'Jesus Christ heals you!' And so can we! Yes, we can practice the same power and authority in prayer: we can speak against obstacles and hindrances in the spiritual realm when we speak in the name of Jesus. Didn't Jesus even tell us to speak to the mountain?

> *For verily I say unto you, That whosoever shall say unto this mountain, Be thou removed, and be thou cast into the sea; and shall not doubt in his heart, but shall believe that those things which he says shall come to pass; he shall have whatsoever he says. (Mark 11:23, KJV).*

What we are told here is to 'speak to your mountain' in the name of Jesus. Speak to your hindrance in the spiritual realm in the name of Jesus. Or if there is a hindrance in the visible realm, speak to the spiritual 'mountain' or 'cause' that is behind it! Command it to leave. Tell it, 'be though removed', in the name of Jesus.

When we minister to people's needs through the laying on of hands, we must use the name of Jesus and exercise the power and authority in His name into the particular need or situation. And the same must apply when we pray for people from the pulpit.

In a very large scale, the church has not exercised her authority yet. She has just asked God in prayer. When the church really starts to realize that she is entrusted with the name of Jesus and starts to exercise the power and authority that comes with that name, there will be another spiritual revolution since this is exactly what the Apostles did as recorded in The Book of Acts. This is one of their main keys to the tremendous breakthroughs and victories they experienced. A compromise in this matter will not work. To obtain similar results, we must practice the same as they did. If we keep approaching God (or just ask Him to deal with the enemy) without approaching the enemy ourselves, we will go nowhere. We will just go in circles. No church growth principles or social studies will help if we don't approach and deal with the enemy in Jesus' name. If fasting and prayer are practiced without exercising the power and authority in the name of Jesus, fasting and prayer will only have limited effect or no effect at all.

People pray but don't obtain the desired victory or results. They then very often think that if they can be sanctified enough, then their prayers will be more powerful. Other people think that if they can improve their behavior enough, then their prayers will be more effective. Some people think that if they just can fast more or repent more, then their prayers will obtain more results. Many more think that if they can fulfill certain conditions that would make them deserve God's answer to prayer, then they will really have a breakthrough. None of these methods will help. Such thinking is based on the lack of understanding of God's Word and grace. Some people try to defeat the enemy and obtain victory over him by their own efforts in prayer. We could go on and on.

Obviously, we are in no way speaking against fasting, prayer, good behavior, repentance or giving. What we are pointing to is the danger of these things becoming substitutes for God's grace and the blood of Jesus. We are also pointing to the failure that can be caused by practicing prayer, fasting, repentance and giving without exercising the power and authority in the name of Jesus for the healing of the sick and against the enemy.

The fact is that victory and answer to prayer are based on God's grace. We were not worthy, but Christ is worthy, and through Him God has made us worthy. It is all based on grace and nothing else.

Jesus has already defeated the enemy through his own victory on the cross:

> *Blotting out the handwriting of ordinances that was against us, which was contrary to us, and took it out of the way, nailing it to his cross; And having spoiled principalities and powers, he made a show of them openly, triumphing over them in it.*
> *(Colossians 2:14-15, KJV).*

He nailed that which was against and contrary to us to the cross, and 'spoiled the principalities and powers' in it. He defeated the evil 'principalities and powers in heavenly places.'

> *Forasmuch then as the children are partakers of flesh and blood,*
> *he also himself likewise took part of the same; that through death*

he might destroy him that had the power of death, that is, the devil. (Hebrews 2:14, KJV).

Through His resurrection, He has enforced and guaranteed this victory forever. Now, He has given this victory to us. He has given us authority over the enemy in His own name, the name of Jesus Christ of Nazareth! You and I are now entrusted with that name. It is time we took advantage of this and started using it as Christ's representatives!

4.2. The keys of the kingdom of heaven

It is obvious that some very special authority was given to the apostle Peter:

> *You are Peter, a rock. This is the rock on which I will put together my church, a church so expansive with energy that not even the gates of hell will be able to keep it out. And that's not all. You will have complete and free access to God's kingdom, keys to open any and every door: no more barriers between heaven and earth, earth and heaven. A yes on earth is yes in heaven. A 'no' on earth is a 'no' in heaven. (Matthew 16:18b, 19, MSG).*

> *And I will give you the keys of the kingdom of heaven, and whatever you bind on earth will be bound in heaven, and whatever you loose on earth will be loosed in heaven. (Matthew 16:19, NKJV).*

Jesus gave the keys to Peter. These keys can be used both to bind (lock) and to loose (open up). Peter used this apostolic authority to open up (loose) on the day of Pentecost (Acts 2) as well as in the house of Cornelius (Acts 10).

On the day of Pentecost, the first part of the church was established, composed only of the Jews (or the people of Israel). In Cornelius' house, the door of the kingdom of heaven was opened to the Gentiles. That's how the first part of the Gentile church was established. In the first case, Peter used the loosing power of the keys for the Jews, or people of Israel; in the second case he used their losing power towards the Gentiles.

4.3.   Through Peter, this authority did not leave the church

The authority and the keys of the kingdom of heaven did not leave the earth and the church.

As Jesus gives Peter the keys, He says to Peter: "whatever you bind on earth will be bound in heaven, and whatever you loose on earth will be loosed in heaven." He is, of course, referring to the use of the keys. For example, if you have a lock, a chain and a key, you can use the key to bind someone with the chain. Therefore, Binding and loosing requires the keys of the kingdom of heaven.

> *Let the high praises of God be in their mouth, And a two-edged sword in their hand, To execute vengeance on the nations, And punishments on the peoples; To **bind** their kings **with chains**, And their nobles with fetters of iron; To*

execute on them the written judgment – his honor have all
His saints. (Psalm 149:6-9, NKJV).

The expression "whatever you bind on earth will be bound in heaven, and whatever you loose on earth will be loosed in heaven" is also used in Matthew 18:18. Let us read it in its context:

> *But if he will not hear thee, then take with thee one or two more, that in the mouth of two or three witnesses every word may be established. And if he shall neglect to hear them, **tell it unto the church**: but if he neglects to hear the church, let him be unto thee as a heathen man and a publican. Verily I say unto you, whatsoever ye shall bind on earth shall be bound in heaven: and whatsoever ye shall loose on earth shall be loosed in heaven.*
> *(Matthew 18:16-19, KJV).*

In the above verses, we can easily see that 'the church' is given the authority to 'bind and loose'. Therefore, the keys of the kingdom of heaven are present in the church today. The church is given authority. It is impossible to perform such binding and loosing without the possession of 'the keys of the kingdom of heaven'.

4.4. Jesus gave authority to His disciples and followers

> *For the Son of Man is as a man taking a far journey, who left his house, and gave authority to his servants, and to every man his work, and commanded the porter to watch.*
> *(Mark 13:34, KJV).*

Jesus would not have given His disciples this authority if it was not necessary. It is impossible to cast out demons without having authority over them. In a similar way, it is impossible to perform healings by the power of God without being authorized to do so.

4.5. Two ministries for every believer

There are two ministries in which every believer participates. In fact, all believers have the ministry of a king and of a priest:

Despite that, not all believers have the ministry or office of an apostle, or of a prophet or of an evangelist or so on.

Many believers have the feeling that some believers are priests and some believers are kings. They believe, as was the case under the old covenant, that we cannot be kings and priests at the same time. But there seems to be no evidence for that interpretation of the Scriptures. The Bible teaches that Jesus is King and Priest at the same time, in line with Melchizedek (Genesis 14:18). The Bible uses the expression, 'a' royal priesthood. That is to say, one royal priesthood! This does not sound as if we are being divided into one group of kings and one group of priests:

> *But you are a chosen race, **a royal priesthood,** a dedicated nation, [God's] own purchased, special people, that you may set forth the wonderful deeds and display the virtues and perfections of Him Who called you out of darkness into His marvelous light. (1 Peter 2:9, AMP).*

As believers, we are authorized through the ministry and office of a king and a priest. It is the anointing received for these two particular ministries that authorize every believer to take part in the royal as well as the priestly authority. In our case, the anointing is, of course, that of the Holy Spirit: the anointing with the Holy Spirit and with power. As we have seen previously, in Acts 10:38, Jesus was authorized, that is, anointed with the Holy Spirit and with power. A Bible verse stresses this out:

> *But you shall receive power when the Holy Spirit has come upon you; and you shall be witnesses to Me in Jerusalem, and in all Judea and Samaria, and to the end of the earth. (Acts 1:8, NKJV).*

The first Bible verse (Acts 10:38) refers to Jesus. The second one (Acts 1:8) refers to the Church or the believers.

CHAPTER V
HEALING MIRACLES, SIGNS, WONDERS, VICTORY, HARVEST IN TODAY'S CHURCH

5.1. The way for the church to obtain victories

To obtain equivalent effectiveness, victories and results to those found in the Book of Acts, we need the same kind of authority they had. There is no human, natural or substitute for divine authorization. Before we go further, we will give examples of the principle of authorization in the Bible, which are found in the Message Bible version:

> *I, Paul, am a devoted slave of Jesus Christ on assignment,* **authorized as an apostle** *to proclaim God's words and acts. I write this letter to all the believers in Rome, God's friends. (Romans 1:1, MSG).*

> *The fate of Ahaziah when he went to visit was God's judgment on him. When Ahaziah arrived at Jezreel, he and Joram met with Jehu son of Nimshi,* **whom God had already** *authorized* **to destroy the dynasty of Ahab.**
> *(2 Chronicles 22:7a, MSG).*

> **I never sent these prophets, never** *authorized* *a single one of them. (Jeremiah 23:32b, MSG).*

To be a prophet, one must be authorized for the office of a prophet:

As a consequence of the authority that they were given, they had a steady stream of signs, wonders and miracles.

> *I will not venture to speak of anything except what Christ has accomplished through me in leading the Gentiles to obey God by what I have said and done – by the power of signs and miracles, through the power of the Spirit. So from Jerusalem all the way around to Illyricum, I have fully proclaimed the gospel of Christ. (Romans 15:18-19).*

The biblical principle (method) and the key to getting 'the Gentiles to obey God' were 'the power of signs and miracles'. This is the biblical principle we see demonstrated in the Book of Acts. This was the reason for their tremendous success in church growth and soul winning. This is *the* biblical principle, or 'method', (if you prefer to call it that) for spreading the gospel, soul winning and church growth. There is no other biblical way!

In modern days and times, the biblical principle of signs and wonders has been substituted with all kinds of human produced ideas, methods and efforts. Yet, signs and wonders were the way in the Book of Acts and it is the way today. The biblical principle can never be changed. It cannot be substituted by anything else. If we do not acknowledge this truth and act accordingly, we shall always experience the uttermost failure. "To the word and to the testimony!" People who try other ways get nowhere:

Tell them, 'No, we're going to study the Scriptures.' People who try the other ways get nowhere – a dead end! Frustrated and famished, they try one thing after another. When nothing works out they get angry, cursing first this god and then that one, Looking this way and that, up, down, and sideways – and seeing nothing, A blank wall, an empty hole. They end up in the dark with nothing. (Isaiah 8:19-22, MSG).

Here is what 'the word and the testimony,' the Scriptures say:

And my speech and my preaching were not with persuasive words of human wisdom, but in **demonstration of the Spirit and of power**, *that your faith should not be in the wisdom of men but in the power of God. (1 Corinthians 2:4-5, NKJV).*

How shall we escape if we neglect so great a salvation, which at the first began to be spoken by the Lord, and was confirmed to us by those who heard Him, God also bearing **witness both with signs and wonders, with various miracles**, *and gifts of the Holy Spirit, according to His own will? (Hebrews 2:3-4, NKJV).*

The servants of God who operated with such tremendous power, signs, wonders and effectiveness did so with authority: they were sent by God! They had their authority from Him. This was the way in the Book of Acts, and it is still the way today. And now, let's remember this:

If we have sown spiritual things for you, is it a great thing if we reap your material things?
(1 Corinthians 9:11, NKJV).

And let him who is instructed in the word share with him who is instructing – in all good things.
(Galatians 6:6, YLT).

5.2. Operating with authority

God does not entrust just anybody with His power. But some are entrusted with it. Another way to say this is that He has authorized them. If someone is anointed, it means that they are authorized. And any believer of Christ is anointed:

> *Now He who establishes us with you in Christ **and has anointed** us is God, who also has sealed us and given us the Spirit in our hearts as a guarantee.*
> *(2 Corinthians 1:21-22, NKJV).*

We could say, 'He who establishes us... and has authorized us is God':

> *But **you have an anointing from the Holy One**, and you know all things. (1 John 2:20, NKJV).*

Now we could say, 'You have an authorization from the Holy One':

> *But **the anointing which you have received from Him abides in you**, and you do not need that anyone teach you; but as the same anointing teaches you concerning all things, and is true, and is not a lie, and just as it has taught you, you will abide in Him. (1 John 2:27, NKJV).*

Also, we could say that 'the authorization which you received from Him abides in you' because every believer is anointed, every believer is authorized. There is something available in addition to 'the anointing that abides *in* you' (1 John 2:27). As previously mentioned, "God anointed Jesus of Nazareth with the Holy Spirit and with power" (Acts 10:38). Moreover, Jesus said: "you shall receive power when the Holy Spirit comes upon you" (Acts 1:8). For that reason, there is an anointing (that is, *authorization,*) 'with the Holy Spirit and with power' for the believers (that is, for the body of Christ). The Anointing was not for Jesus only:

> *Nevertheless, I tell you the truth. It is to your advantage that I go away; for if I do not go away, the Helper will not come to you; but if I depart, I will send Him to you. (John 16:7, NKJV).*

'The Helper' is the Holy Spirit. Remember that the anointing is with *the Holy Spirit* (and with power). In the Book of Acts, after the day of Pentecost and after the Gentiles received salvation and the Holy Spirit in Cornelius' house, the Holy Spirit was received through the laying on of hands of the apostles:

> *They sent Peter and John to them, who, when they had come down, prayed for them that they might receive the Holy Spirit ... Then **they laid hands on them, and they received the Holy Spirit.** (Acts 8:14b-15, 17, NKJV).*

They were anointed with the Holy Spirit through the laying on of hands. They were authorized through the laying on of hands by the apostles:

> *And **when Paul had laid hands on them**, the Holy Spirit came upon them, and they spoke with tongues and prophesied. (Acts 19:6, NKJV).*

This anointing or authorization with the Holy Spirit and with power through the laying on of hands is still available nowadays.

One of the main keys to the tremendous success and victories of the Book of Acts was indeed the apostolic authority:

> Truly **the signs of an apostle** were accomplished among you with all perseverance, in signs and wonders and mighty deeds. *(2 Corinthians 12:12, NKJV).*

> Then fear came upon every soul, and many wonders and signs were done through the **apostles.** *(Acts 2:43, NKJV).*

> And through the hands of the **apostles,** many signs and wonders were done among the people.
> *(Acts 5:12a, NKJV).*

> Now when Simon saw that **the Spirit was bestowed through the laying on of the apostles' hands,** he offered them money, saying, 'Give this **authority** [Greek: eksousian] to me as well, so that everyone on whom I lay my hands may receive the Holy Spirit.'
> *(Acts 8:18-19, NASB).*

> Paul, an **apostle** (not from men nor through man, but through Jesus Christ and God the Father who raised Him from the dead). *(Galatians 1:1, NKJV).*

> And don't tell me that I have no authority to write like this. I'm perfectly free to do this—isn't that obvious? Haven't I been given a job to do? Wasn't I commissioned to this work in a face-to-face meeting with Jesus, our Master? Aren't you yourselves proof of the good work that I've done for the Master? Even if no one else admits **the authority of my commission**, you can't deny it. Why, my work with you is living proof of **my authority**!
> *(1 Corinthians 9:1-2, MSG).*

CHAPTER VI
THE NAME OF JESUS:
AN INHERITANCE

6.1. Meaning of the expression 'in the name of Jesus'

Let's explain this through the Bible:

> *So we are Christ's ambassadors, God making His appeal*
> *as it were through us. We [as Christ's personal*
> *representatives] beg you for His sake to lay hold of the*
> *divine favor [now offered you] and be reconciled to God.*
> *(2 Corinthians 5:20, AMP).*

We are clearly told that we are Christ's personal representatives. In other words, we can operate representatively, on Christ's behalf. Therefore, we may conclude that everywhere the expression* 'in the name of Jesus', or 'in My name', etc. appear in the New Testament of the Bible, they actually mean 'representatively, on Christ's behalf.'

Now, that we know this, we should have a much clearer understanding of what these expressions* really entail.

Let us find a few examples:

> *And these signs will follow those who believe: In My name*
> *they will cast out demons; they will speak with new*
> *tongues. (Mark 16:17, NKJ).*

We should understand this as follows: 'and these signs shall follow them that believe: representatively, on my behalf, they will cast out demons'.

If you ask anything in My name, I will do it. (John 14:14).

We would say: 'if you ask anything, representatively, on my behalf, I will do it'. Another way to say the same thing would be:

And these signs shall follow them that believe: On My authority, they shall cast out demons (Mark 16:17)" and
"If you ask anything on My authority, I will do it
(John 14:14).

When we serve the Lord, we do not operate representing ourselves, on our own behalf or on our own authority. If that were the case, we would actually be trying to serve the Lord in our own name. On the contrary, we operate representatively on Christ's behalf; on His authority when we serve the Lord (this also includes serving the Lord in prayer). This is what it means to operate in His name.

6.2. Implications of the expressions 'in My name', 'in the name of Jesus'

It is of crucial importance for us to understand what is implied by the phrase 'in My name', 'in His name', and 'in the name of Jesus Christ', etc. This is absolutely necessary if we want to effectively take advantage of the fact that we are entrusted with the name of Jesus and its use.

First of all, let's compare a Spanish translation of the Bible with an English translation for the purpose of explanation and understanding:

- ***English version:***
  Now then we are ambassadors for Christ, as though God did beseech you by us: we pray you in Christ's stead, be ye reconciled to God. (2 Corinthians 5:20, KJV).

- ***Spanish version:***
  Así que, somos embajadores en nombre de Cristo, como si Dios rogase por medio nuestro; os rogamos en nombre de Cristo: Reconciliaos con Dios. (2 Corintios 5:20, Reina-Valera Antigua).

Where the English text says, 'for Christ' and 'in Christ's stead', the Spanish text says *'en nombre de Cristo'* in both places, which means 'in (the) name of Christ.'

In a literal translation into English, the Spanish version will read as this: 'Now then we are ambassadors in the name of Christ, as though God did beseech you by us: we beg you in the name of Christ: Be you reconciled to God.' We therefore conclude that 'in Christ's name' means 'for Christ' and 'in Christ's stead'. And this is confirmed in the Bible verse below:

> *So we are Christ's ambassadors, God making His appeal as it were through us. We [as Christ's personal representatives] beg you for His sake to lay hold of the divine favor [now offered you] and be reconciled to God. (2 Corinthians 5:20, AMP).*

An ambassador is a legally authorized representative of the nation that has sent him. Christ has sent us, so we are his legally authorized, personal representatives. A representative acts representatively on behalf of the one he represents. Let's explain this through two Bible verses:

> *For where two or three are gathered together in my name, there am I in the midst of them. (Matthew 18:20, KJV).*

We could then read this verse like this: 'where two or three are gathered together in My stead, representatively on My behalf, there I am in the midst of them.'

> *But Jesus said, Forbid him not: for there is no man which shall do a miracle in my name, that can lightly speak evil of me. (Mark 9:39, KJV).*

This verse could be read like this: 'there is no man who shall do a miracle in My stead, representatively on My behalf, that can easily speak evil of me.'

Now, let's look at the example of Jesus to get further light on this topic:

> *I have come in My Father's name and with His power, and you do not receive Me [your hearts are not open to Me, you give Me no welcome]; but if another comes in his own name and his own power and with no other authority but himself, you will receive him and give him your approval. (John 5:43, AMP).*

Jesus is simply saying that He has not come in His own name, in His own power, in His own authority. He has not come on His own behalf with his own purposes. In the contrary, He has come in His Father's name, power and authority! He has come on His Father's behalf to serve the Father's purposes:

> *Jesus answered them, I told you, and ye believed not: the works that I do in my Father's **name**, they bear witness of me. (John 10:25, AKJV).*

This is the secret to Jesus' effectiveness in doing such works. It is His secret to the miracles He performed. The secret is the name of the Father! He was anointed and authorized with that name and to use that name. When He used the name of the Father to perform these mighty works and miracles, the secret was this: He did not operate in His own power, authority and did not come for his own purposes. Therefore, He was effective when He spoke in His Father's name. In the same manner, we must not operate in our own name. Even if we try to use His name, but, in reality, come in our own name, it is not effective: God has given us the legal right to use the name of Jesus and to speak in that name. But if, in reality, we operate in our own power and authority and for our own purposes, we will be like "a noisy gong or a clanging cymbal" (1 Corinthians 13:1, AMP).

Thus, we understand why it is important that, when we are gathered together, we are really gathered in the name of Jesus:

> *For where two or three are gathered together in My name, I am there in the midst of them. (Matthew 18:20, NKJV).*

It is not sufficient to quote this Bible verse only. Even if we keep on quoting it repeatedly it is of no use if we, in reality, come in our own name so to speak. There are two conditions that must be fulfilled first. And when these two conditions are fulfilled, we are truly gathered in His name and He is truly in our midst:

1. We must be gathered together on His authority;
2. We must not be gathered together in our own name.

If we do not want this authority, we cannot experience the fullness of Christ's presence. And, we cannot operate effectively in His name either.

> *If any man desires to do His will (God's pleasure), he will know (have the needed illumination to recognize, and can tell for himself) whether the teaching is from God or **whether I am speaking from Myself and of My own accord and on My own authority**. (John 7:17, AMP).*

We could possibly paraphrase it like this: 'whether the teaching is in God's name or in my own name...' So, our preaching and teaching must be in the name of Jesus!

Let us now look at the connection between 'in the name of Jesus' and authority in various Bible versions:

> *And when He entered the sacred enclosure of the temple, the chief priests and elders of the people came up to Him as He was teaching and said, **By what power of authority** are You doing these things, and who gave You this power of authority? (Matthew 21:23, AMP).*

In Acts 4:7, in the Amplified version, we find that *"by what name have you done this"*, is actually translated with: *"by what kind of authority did you do this"*:

> *And they set the men in their midst and repeatedly demanded, By what sort of power or by* **what kind of authority** *did [such people as] you do this [healing]? (Acts 4:7, AMP).*

Now, compare with the New King James Version:

> *And when they had set them in the midst, they asked, 'By what power or by* **what name** *have you done this?' (Acts 4:7, NKJV).*

Notice the connection between '(in the) *name*' and '*authority*' in the following Bible verses:

> *Let it be known and understood by all of you, and by the whole house of Israel, that in the* **name and through the power and authority** *of Jesus Christ of Nazareth, Whom you crucified, [but] Whom God raised from the dead, in Him and by means of Him this man is standing here before you well and sound in body. (Acts 4:10, AMP).*

> *While You stretch out Your hand to cure and to perform signs and wonders through the* **authority and by the power of the name** *of Your holy Child and Servant Jesus. (Acts 4:30, AMP).*

> *Now we charge you, brethren,* **in the name and on the authority** *of our Lord Jesus Christ (the Messiah) that you withdraw and keep away from every brother (fellow believer) who is slack in the performance of duty and is disorderly, living as a shirker and not walking in accord with the traditions and instructions that you have received from us. (2 Thessalonians 3:6, AMP).*

Notice that The Message version uses "*authorized* by my Father" where the King James Version says "in my Father's name":

> *Jesus answered, 'I told you, but you don't believe. Everything I have done has **been** authorized **by my Father**, actions that speak louder than words.'*
> *(John 10:25, MSG).*

> *Jesus answered them, I told you, and ye believed not: the works that I do **in** my **Father's name**, they bear witness of me. (John 10:25, KJV).*

6.3. Co-heirs with Christ

We are joint-heirs with Christ as seen in the following two verses:

> *Having become so much better than the angels, as He has by inheritance obtained a more excellent name than they. (Hebrews 1:4, NKJV).*

> *And if children, then heirs – heirs of God and joint heirs with Christ, if indeed we suffer with Him, that we may also be glorified together. (Romans 8:17, NKJV).*

God has entrusted us with the name of Jesus. Testament and covenant are spoken of as the same thing:

> *For where there is a testament, there must also of necessity be the death of the testator. For a **testament** is in force after men are dead, since it has no power at all while the testator lives. Therefore not even the first **covenant** was dedicated without blood. For when Moses had spoken every precept to all the people according to the law, he took the blood of calves and goats, with water, scarlet wool, and hyssop, and sprinkled both, the book*

*itself and all the people, saying, 'This is the blood of the
covenant which God has commanded you.'
(Hebrews 9:16-20, NKJV).*

As we can see from this Bible passage, testament or covenant in the biblical context is legally based. The testator is Jesus. And He is declared dead. Yet, the fact that He is also risen does not affect the power of the testament. In short, because Jesus died, the testament or the covenant is in force.

The New Covenant also known as The New Testament, with all its promises and inheritance, is dedicated and consecrated through the blood of Jesus. Authorization (the authorization to use and operate in the name of Jesus) is a part of this covenant with its inheritance and promises. Therefore, it legally belongs to every child of God. And it is sealed and guaranteed by the blood of Jesus, which is also called the blood of the eternal *covenant*:

*May the God of peace, who through the blood of the
eternal* **covenant** *brought back from the dead our Lord
Jesus, that great Shepherd of the sheep.
(Hebrews 13:20, NIV).*

6.4. The blood of the covenant

To understand the impact of the blood of the covenant, the notion of 'legal power' implies in a covenant needs to be removed here:

*Of how much worse punishment, do you suppose, will he
be thought worthy who has trampled the Son of God*

*underfoot, counted **the blood of the covenant** by which he was sanctified a common thing, and insulted the Spirit of grace? (Hebrews 10:29, NKJV).*

*And He said to them, This is My blood of the new **covenant**, which is shed for many. (Mark 14:24, NKJV).*

We are authorized by commission because the Great Commission is a part of this covenant:

And Jesus came and spoke to them, saying, "All authority has been given to Me in heaven and on earth. Go therefore and make disciples of all the nations, baptizing them in the name of the Father and of the Son and of the Holy Spirit, teaching them to observe all things that I have commanded you; and lo, I am with you always, even to the end of the age." Amen. (Mathew 28:18-20, NKJV).

And He said to them, "Go into all the world and preach the gospel to every creature. He who believes and is baptized will be saved; but he who does not believe will be condemned. And these signs will follow those who believe: In My name they will cast out demons; they will speak with new tongues; they will take up serpents; and if they drink anything deadly, it will by no means hurt them; they will lay hands on the sick, and they will recover." (Mark 16:15-18, NKJV).

With the Great Commission comes the availability of Christ's authority, the right to use the name of Jesus, to cast out devils and heal the sick. In other parts of the Bible, we are also told that God has entrusted us with responsibilities and tasks.

6.5. Implications of being Christ's representatives

As stated previously, we operate in someone else's name, in the name of Jesus, because we have been given the authority to act on His behalf:

> *We are therefore Christ's ambassadors, as though God were making his appeal through us. We implore you **on Christ's behalf**: Be reconciled to God.*
> *(2 Corinthians 5:20, NIV).*

> ***We're Christ's representatives****. God uses us to persuade men and women to drop their differences and enter into God's work of making things right between them. We're speaking for Christ himself now: Become friends with God; he's already a friend with you.*
> *(2 Corinthians 5:20, MSG).*

It would be completely unlawful to operate in someone else's name (that is, on someone else's behalf) without first being in possession of the legal right to do so. Before the now four-digit pin code took over in the banking system, we used to show our debit or credit cards and write down our signature on a paper. As a consequence, the money was transferred from our bank account automatically to pay for goods and services. Nowadays, if we go to a cash point to pay, we don't necessarily give our signature, but we can use a four-digit code instead. Therefore, the four-digit code represents our signature. But if someone got hold of our four-digit pin code after stealing or finding our debit or credit card, we might say they were operating in our name. But the fact is, they were lacking the legal backing to use it. Actually, even though they would operate 'in our name', what they did, would be completely illegal.

6.6. Operating in the name of Jesus: a provision for every Christian

As a believer, you have authority to cast out the enemy:

> *And these signs shall follow them that believe; In my name shall they cast out devils. (Mark 16:17a, KJV).*

You may remind the enemy of Christ's victory through His death and resurrection. Then you can command the enemy to leave. By giving this commandment in the name of Jesus Christ, you stamp your order and commandment against the enemy with the legal valid signature of Jesus Christ. The enemy has lost his right. He has to leave. But if you don't know that, or if you don't know the authority you have over him in Jesus' name, the enemy will take advantage of this and try to stay where he is.

According to God's Word and promises you can approach God the Father through the name of Jesus. You can also use the name of Jesus against the enemy according to the same Word and promises. This is all yours. It is your legal right. In other words, you have the authority (you are authorized) to use the name of Jesus.

Now, look at an example when some people tried to use the name of Jesus against evil powers without being authorized to do so:

> *Then certain of the vagabond Jews, exorcists, took upon them to call over them which had evil spirits the name of the LORD Jesus, saying, We adjure you by Jesus whom Paul preaches. And there were seven sons of one Sceva, a Jew, and chief of the priests, which did so. And the evil spirit answered and said, Jesus I know, and Paul I know; but who are ye? And the man in whom the evil spirit was leaped on them, and overcame them, and prevailed against them, so that they fled out of that house naked and wounded. And this was known to all the Jews and Greeks also dwelling at Ephesus; and fear fell on them all, and the name of the Lord Jesus was magnified.*
> *(Acts 19:13-17, KJV).*

These exorcists were operating in someone else's name without being legally authorized to do so. We think it is reasonable to believe that these exorcists previously must have had some kind of success in exorcising evil spirits. They most probably had operated in some degree of Adamic power. But now they were in for a big surprise! They had seen and observed the apostle Paul getting the spirits out without performing any kind of 'rituals', 'magic' or 'exorcism'. There were no long fasting or nightlong prayers. Of course, here there is no insinuation that Paul didn't pray or fast a lot. What we are saying is that he didn't start prayer and fasting to get the spirits out when he was confronted with them.

These exorcists mentioned in Acts 19 had seen and observed the apostle, who was operating from a position of authority. Jesus had already defeated these evil spirits. Now Paul was exercising authority over them. He spoke in the name of Jesus and just ordered the spirits out. The exorcists had probably never seen anything like that before. They must have been amazed by Paul. Needless to recall that Paul represented the kingdom of God. He was bringing in the rule of God's kingdom on earth. This was not the case when these exorcists exorcized evil spirits. Now, they tried to use the name of Jesus. But they did not have the legal right and authority to use that name. Thus, when the evil spirits heard the name of Jesus, they might have been greatly disturbed. So, they jumped on the exorcists and the name of Jesus was magnified.

CHAPTER VII
THE VICTORY OF CHRIST, THE CAUSE OF THE AUTHORITY

7.1. Jesus gave us authority over the enemy

The church has authority over the enemy; every believer has authority over the enemy.

> *God wiped out the charges that were against us for disobeying the Law of Moses. He took them away and nailed them to **the cross**. *There Christ defeated all powers and forces. He let the whole world see them being led away as prisoners when he celebrated his victory. (Colossians 2:14-15, CEV).*

> *[God] disarmed the principalities and powers that were ranged against us and made a bold display and public example of them, in triumphing over them in Him and in it [the cross**]. (Colossians 2:15, AMP).*

Please be aware that '***there*** Christ defeated' and 'triumphing over them in it [***the cross*****]' are conclusions made by the translators. They are not in the original language. Let's then look into the literal translation:

> *Having stripped the principalities and the authorities, he made a shew of them openly – having triumphed over them in it (Greek: auto).* (Colossians 2:15, YLT).*

*The Greek word *'autos'* can be defined both as he [or him], she and it, as well as they, them and [the] same.[2]

The original translation literary says, "having triumphed over them in *it* [alternatively: 'in him' or in the 'same' 'The same' here in this context, grammatically would refer to 'the cross [or possible to 'him']" (see Colossians 2:15, AMP).

7.2. Jesus defeated the devil through his death

> *Since therefore the children partake of blood and flesh, he also, in like manner, took part in the same, that **through death he might annul him who has the might of death**, that is, the devil. (Hebrews 2:14, DARBY).*

This Bible verse shows us that the physical death of Jesus was necessary to defeat the devil. Through Jesus' physical death, His blood was shed. Through his death, He annulled him, the devil. Furthermore, He defeated, disarmed and triumphed over all the evil, *"principalities and powers in the heavenly places"* (Ephesians 3:10). All this was a consequence of the total obedience of Jesus to the Father on the cross.

7.3. Jesus was obedient unto His death on the cross

---

[2] See Strong's Concordance/ [http://biblehub.com].

<blockquote>
Let this same attitude and purpose and [humble] mind be in you which was in Christ Jesus: [Let Him be your example in humility:] Who, although being essentially one with God and in the form of God [possessing the fullness of the attributes which make God God], did not think this equality with God was a thing to be eagerly grasped or retained, But stripped Himself [of all privileges and rightful dignity], so as to assume the guise of a servant (slave), in that He became like men and was born a human being. And after He had appeared in human form, He abased and humbled Himself [still further] and carried His obedience to the extreme of death, even the death of the cross! (Philippians 2:5-8, AMP).
</blockquote>

Because of this complete victory on the cross, God has exalted Him and set Him at His right hand:

<blockquote>
And after He had appeared in human form, He abased and humbled Himself [still further] and carried His obedience to the extreme of death, even the death of the cross! Therefore [because He stooped so low] God has highly exalted Him and has freely bestowed on Him the name that is above every name, That in (at) the name of Jesus every knee should (must) bow, in heaven and on earth and under the earth, And every tongue frankly and openly confess and acknowledge that Jesus Christ is Lord, to the glory of God the Father.
(Philippians 2:8-12, AMP).
</blockquote>

Because of His mighty victory at the cross, the name of Jesus had now become the name that is above every name. Not only that! But all evil spirits and powers, in the heavenly places, on earth and in the underworld have to give in to His name!

<blockquote>
That in the name of Jesus every knee should bow in heaven on earth and under the earth.
(Philippians 2:10, NIV).
</blockquote>

Compare this verse with the following passage from the Bible:

> *Which He worked in Christ when He raised Him from the dead and seated Him at His right hand in the heavenly places, far above all principality and power and might and dominion, and every name that is named, not only in this age but also in that which is to come And He put all things under His feet, and gave Him to be head over all things to the church. (Ephesians 1:20-22, NKJV).*

Through His obedience, death and resurrection all these evil principalities and powers were completely defeated. As a consequence, they were put under Christ's feet.

7.4. God has seated us with Jesus

> *And He raised us up together with Him and made us sit down together [giving us joint seating with Him] in the heavenly sphere [by virtue of our being] in Christ Jesus (the Messiah, the Anointed One). (Ephesians 2:6, AMP).*

Literary translation:

> *And did raise [us] up together, and did seat [us] together in the heavenly [places] in Christ Jesus.*
> *(Ephesians 2:6, YLT).*

As a consequence of the fact that we are seated with Him in this position, all these evil principalities and powers are put under our feet now. Therefore, we have complete authority over them. This authority is of course found in the name of Jesus, "the name which is above every name", "in heaven on earth and under the earth."

CONCLUSION

Jesus has defeated the enemy. Because of His victory, the entire enemy's power is placed under His feet. 'We' are seated with Christ in this heavenly position. This refers to the Church. Every believer is included in 'we' in this context. As a consequence, every believer has been given authority over the enemy in the name of Jesus Christ on a legal basis.

We are authorized through predestination, election and calling.

We are authorized because we are chosen.

Now, it is important to bear in mind that election, predestination and calling represent grace (mercy) and are in contrast to human effort – trying to satisfy God and obtain things from Him by the principle of the Law:

> *So too, at the present time there is a remnant* **chosen by grace**. *(Romans 11:5-6, NIV).*

> *And if by grace, then it is no longer by works; if it were, grace would no longer be grace. (Romans 11:7, AMP).*

> *What then [shall we conclude]? Israel failed to obtain what it sought [God's favor by obedience to the Law]. Only* **the** *elect (those chosen few) obtained it, while the rest of them became callously indifferent (blinded, hardened, and made insensible to it).*
> *(Romans 11:7, AMPC).*

> *It does not, therefore, depend on human desire or effort, but on God's mercy. Now to him who works, the wages*

are not counted as grace but as debt. (Romans 9:16, NIVUK).

Therefore, God's choice does not depend on a person's will or effort, but on God himself, who shows mercy. (Romans 9:16, ISV).

Our heavenly position of authority in Christ is not dependent on and is not obtained through human will or effort. A Bible verse that should help us understand this principle of election and grace is the following:

Yet, before the twins were born or had done anything good or bad – in order that God's purpose in election might stand: 12 not by works but by him who calls – she was told, 'The older will serve the younger.'
(Romans 9:11-12, NIV).

Many of God's children are still living in bondage as regards these things. This is very much due to the lack of revelation concerning their heavenly position of authority in Christ. Many believers always think that they haven't prayed enough, they haven't fasted enough and that they must do more spiritual warfare to obtain it. Or, they may think that if they can improve their lifestyle, be successful enough in walking in the Spirit, or be enough sanctified, then they will experience this authority and this special anointing, as much as healings, miracles, signs and wonders will follow them. The truth is that we will never pray enough. We can always improve in walking in the Spirit. We will never be sanctified enough. People think they are not worthy and try their best to improve themselves, hoping to receive a reward from God for their efforts. Such people are living in spiritual bondage:

> *Tell me, you who desire to be under the law, do you not hear the law? For it is written that Abraham had two sons: the one by a bondwoman, the other by a freewoman. But he who was of the bondwoman was born according to the flesh, and he of the freewoman through promise, which things are symbolic. For these are the two covenants: the one from Mount Sinai, which gives birth to bondage, which is Hagar for this Hagar is Mount Sinai in Arabia, and corresponds to Jerusalem which now is, and* **is in bondage with her children.**
> *(Galatians 4:21-25, NKJV).*

Because we were reckoned as useless in trying to please God, there was only one place for us, and that was on the cross:

> *But God forbid that I should boast except in the cross of our Lord Jesus Christ, by whom the world has been crucified to me, and I to the world.*
> *(Galatians 6:14, NKJV).*

This is, of course, an offense to the self-righteous, non-crucified nature:

> *And I, brethren, if I still preach circumcision, why do I still suffer persecution? Then* **the *offense* of the cross** *has ceased. (Galatians 5:11, NKJV).*

But the Good News is that Christ lives in us!

> *I have been crucified with Christ; it is no longer I who live, but Christ lives in me; and the life which I now live in the flesh I live by faith in the Son of God, who loved me and gave Himself for me. (Galatians 2:20, NKJV).*

He fulfills the requirements of the Law in me us:

He condemned sin in the flesh, that the righteous requirement of the law might be fulfilled in us who do not walk according to the flesh but according to the Spirit. (Romans 8:3b-4, NKJV).

He holds the authority of God because He is the authorized One; He is the anointed One:

To them, God willed to make known what are the riches of the glory of this mystery among the Gentiles: which is Christ in you, the hope of glory. (Colossians 1:27, NKJV).

He manifests God's glory. And He manifests the authority of God through us. Praise His name! What a wonderful rest and what a wonderful joy!

On a hill far away stood an old rugged cross,
The emblem of suffering and shame;
And I love that old cross where the dearest and best
For a world of lost sinners was slain.

O that old rugged cross, so despised by the world,
Has a wondrous attraction for me;
For the dear Lamb of God left His glory above
To pardon and sanctify me.[3]

*For I determined not to know anything among you except Jesus Christ **and Him crucified**. I was with you in weakness, in fear, and in much trembling. And my speech and my preaching were not with persuasive words of human wisdom, but in demonstration of the Spirit and of power, that your faith should not be in the wisdom of men but in the power of God. (1 Corinthians 2:2-5, NKJV).*

---

[3] (George Bennard)
http://library.timelesstruths.org/music/The_Old_Rugged_Cross/

> *This only I want to learn from you: Did you receive the Spirit by the works of the law, or by the hearing of faith? Therefore, He who supplies the Spirit to you and works miracles among you, does He do it by the works of the law, or by the hearing of faith? (Galatians 3:2-5, NKJV).*

Let's sum up: because we are authorized with the anointing, we have the Holy Spirit and power. The Holy Spirit and the power are the evidence. If there is no Spirit, there is no authority. If there is no power, there is no authority either:

> *But I will come to you shortly, if the Lord wills, and I will know, not the word of those who are puffed up, **but the power.** For the kingdom of God is not in word but in power. (1 Corinthians 4:19-20, NKJV).*

All in all, we are authorized:

- through the anointing
- through the ministry
- through the name of Jesus Christ
- through the covenant
- through divine 'Power Of Attorney'
- by commission
- by sending
- by calling
- through predestination (being chosen through election)

INDEX